Languages of the World

Polish

Lucia Raatma

Raintree

www.raintreepublishers.co.uk
Visit our website to find out more information about Raintree books.

To order:
☎ Phone 0845 6044371
🖷 Fax +44 (0) 1865 312263
🖥 Email myorders@raintreepublishers.co.uk

Customers from outside the UK please telephone +44 1865 312262

Raintree is an imprint of Capstone Global Library Limited, a company incorporated in England and Wales having its registered office at 7 Pilgrim Street, London, EC4V 6LB – Registered company number: 6695582

Edited by Dan Nunn, Rebecca Rissman, and Catherine Veitch
Designed by Marcus Bell
Picture research by Ruth Blair
Originated by Capstone Global Library
Printed and bound in China by South China Printing Company Ltd

ISBN 978 1 406 22452 8 (hardback)
15 14 13 12 11
10 9 8 7 6 5 4 3 2 1

ISBN 978 1 406 22459 7 (paperback)
16 15 14 13 12
10 9 8 7 6 5 4 3 2 1

British Library Cataloguing in Publication Data
Raatma, Lucia.
Polish. -- (Languages of the world)
491.8'5-dc22
A full catalogue record for this book is available from the British Library.

Acknowledgements
We would like to thank the following for permission to reproduce photographs: Alamy pp. 5 (© Julio Etchart), 7 (© Brigette Sullivan/Outer Focus Photos); Corbis pp. 11 (© Radoslaw Pietruszka/PAP), 22 (© Miroslaw Trembecki/PAP), 24 (© Juan Francisco Moreno/epa), 29 (© Ian Trower/JAI); iStockphoto p. 15 (© Igor Stepovik); Photolibrary pp. 23 (Peter Arkell), 28 (Superstock); Shutterstock pp. 6 (© Monkey Business Images), 8 (© Miau), 9 (© c.), 10 (© blueking), 12 (© Golden Pixels LLC), 13 (© ImageryMajestic), 14 (© jadimages), 16 (© Dmitriy Shironosov), 17 (© Zurijeta), 18 (© katatonia82), 19 (© mkasperski), 20 (© privilege), 21 (© stefanolunardi), 25 (© Stanislaw Tokarski), 26 (© barbaradudzinska), 27 (© Taratorki).

Cover photograph of a young girl reproduced with permission of iStockphoto (© Krystian Kaczmarski).

We would like to thank Dorota Holowiak for her invaluable help in the preparation of this book.

Every effort has been made to contact copyright holders of material reproduced in this book. Any omissions will be rectified in subsequent printings if notice is given to the publisher.

Disclaimer
All the Internet addresses (URLs) given in this book were valid at the time of going to press. However, due to the dynamic nature of the Internet, some addresses may have changed, or sites may have changed or ceased to exist since publication. While the author and publisher regret any inconvenience this may cause readers, no responsibility for any such changes can be accepted by either the author or the publisher.

Contents

Polish words are in italics, *like this*. You can find out how to say them by looking in the pronunciation guide.

Polish around the world

The Polish language is spoken all over the world. It is the main language of Poland. Some people also speak Polish in other countries in Europe such as Slovakia, Ukraine, Russia, and Romania.

Poland

Poland is in Europe.

Many towns in the United Kingdom have Polish shops.

There are many Polish speakers in the United Kingdom and the United States, too. Some people speak Polish in Australia and Brazil as well.

Who speaks Polish?

There are about 40 million Polish speakers in the world. In Poland, nearly everyone speaks Polish. But there are different types, or dialects, of Polish in different parts of the country.

These people are taking part in a Polish festival in Chicago, in the United States.

In the United Kingdom there are about two million people who have a Polish background. Many of them can still speak Polish.

Polish and English

You may already know some Polish words. Many English words are so well known that they are part of the Polish language now. Some examples are *parking, jazz,* and *weekend.*

The word *jazz*, a type of music, is now part of the Polish language.

The English word "parking" has become part of the Polish language.

Some Polish words may sound familiar. See if you can guess what these Polish words mean in English.

lampa   matematyka   mleko   muzyka
(See page 32 for answers.)

Learning Polish

The Polish alphabet is similar to the English alphabet. However, there are no letters q, v, or x. The Polish language also uses special marks called diacritics to make some extra letters.

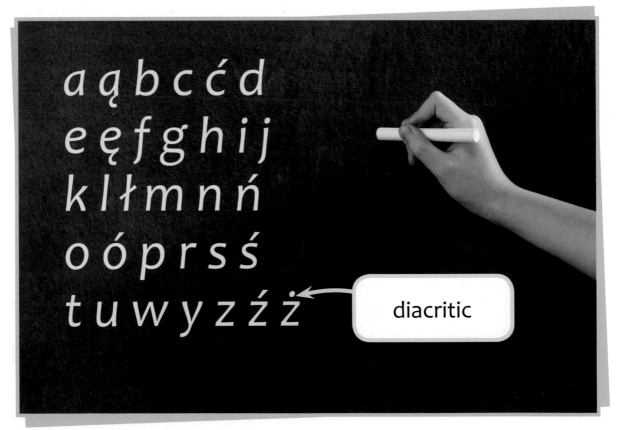

a ą b c ć d
e ę f g h i j
k l ł m n ń
o ó p r s ś
t u w y z ź ż

diacritic

Some letters in Polish are sounded, or pronounced, differently from English. Below are some examples.

c	sounds like "ts"	*co* (what) is pronounced "tsoh"
w	sounds like "v"	*wyspa* (island) is pronounced "vis-pah"
j	sounds like "y"	*jeden* (one) is pronounced "yed-en"
cz	sounds like "ch"	*czas* (time) is pronounced "chahs"

Saying hello and goodbye

In Poland people greet each other in many ways. Some shake hands. Some kiss each others' cheeks or give a hug. Others nod and smile.

How to say it
kiss = *pocałunek*
hug = *uścisk*
smile = *uśmiech*

How to say it
hi = *cześć*
goodnight = *dobranoc*
goodbye = *do widzenia*

Polish speakers might say "*cześć*"
("hi"). At the end of the day people
might say "*do widzenia*" ("goodbye")
or "*dobranoc*" ("goodnight").

Talking about yourself

If you are speaking Polish, the first thing you might do is introduce yourself: *"Mam na imię …"* ("My name is …"). Then you might say to someone *"Bardzo mi miło"* ("Pleased to meet you").

How to say it
My name is … = *Mam na imię …*
Pleased to meet you = *Bardzo mi miło*

How to say it
I speak Polish = *Mówię po polsku*
I do not understand = *Nie rozumiem*

"*Mówię po polsku*" means "I speak Polish". But if someone speaks too quickly you might reply "*Nie rozumiem*" ("I do not understand").

Asking about others

When meeting someone for the first time you might ask, *"Jak masz na imię?"* ("What is your name?") You might also ask *"Skąd jesteś?"* ("Where are you from?")

What is your name? = *Jak masz na imię?*
Where are you from? = *Skąd jesteś?*

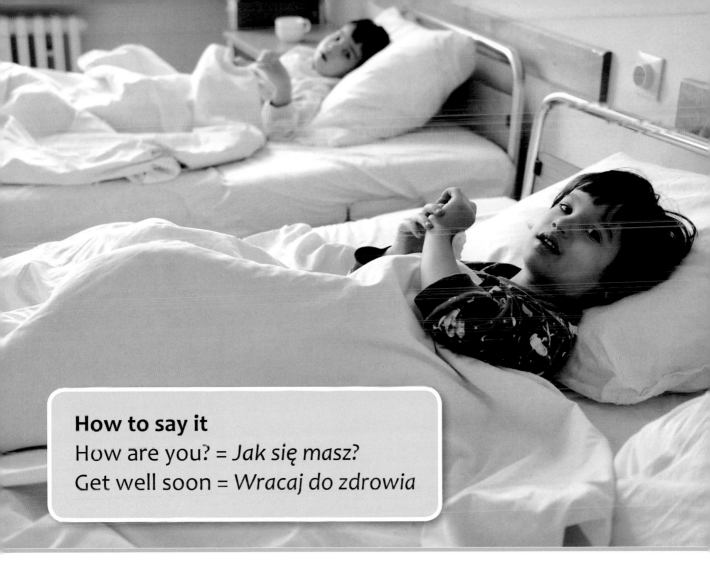

How to say it

How are you? = *Jak się masz?*

Get well soon = *Wracaj do zdrowia*

You might ask a friend or family member *"Jak się masz?"* ("How are you?")
If someone is sick you could say *"Wracaj do zdrowia."* ("Get well soon.")

At home

In Poland people may live in apartments or flats, or in large houses. They might live in big, busy cities such as Kraków or Warsaw.

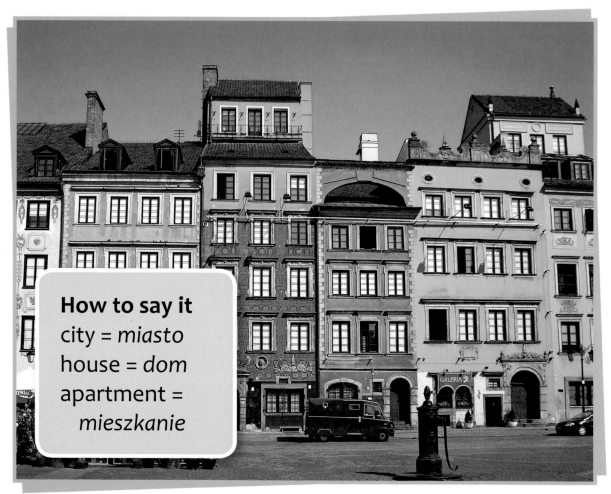

How to say it
city = *miasto*
house = *dom*
apartment =
mieszkanie

How to say it
village = *wioska*
farm = *gospodarstwo*
horse = *koń*
chicken = *kurczę*

Poland also has many villages. People farm the land and grow apples, pears, and plums. They also raise horses, geese, and chickens.

Family life

Families in Poland are like families in many other countries. Often parents and children have other relatives living with them. These might include grandparents or aunts and uncles.

How to say it
father = *ojciec*
mother = *matka*
children = *dzieci*

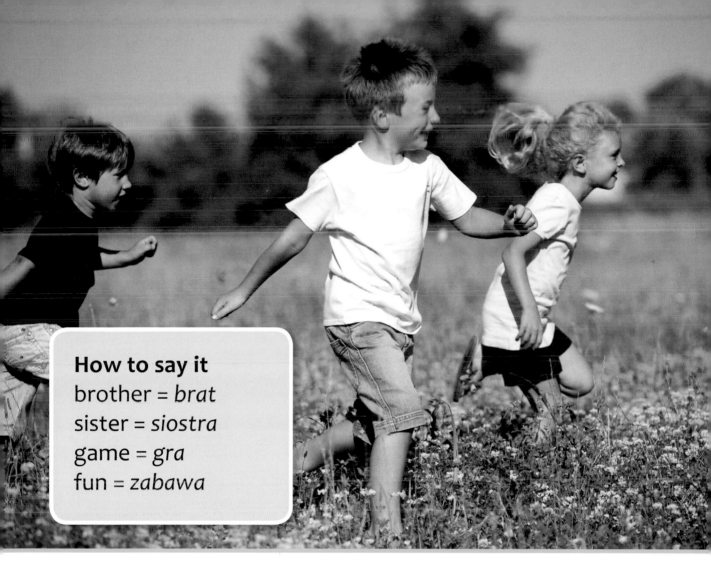

How to say it
brother = *brat*
sister = *siostra*
game = *gra*
fun = *zabawa*

People in Poland enjoy watching television, and using computers and mobile phones. Children enjoy playing outdoor games such as *klasy* and *chłopek*. These games are quite like hopscotch.

At school

Children in Poland have to go to school from the age of 6 to 18. Some of their lessons are in maths, science, and history. They also learn other languages, such as English, German, and Russian.

How to say it
school = *szkoła*
pupil = *uczeń*
school bag = *teczka szkolna*

How to say it
teacher = *nauczyciel*
languages = *języki*
history = *historia*

Polish children learn about famous Polish writers and artists. These include the writer Joseph Conrad and the musician Frederic Chopin.

Sport and dance

People in Poland enjoy football. The national team plays at the Silesian Stadium. Polish people also like to play ice hockey, go cycling, and watch motorcycling (speedway).

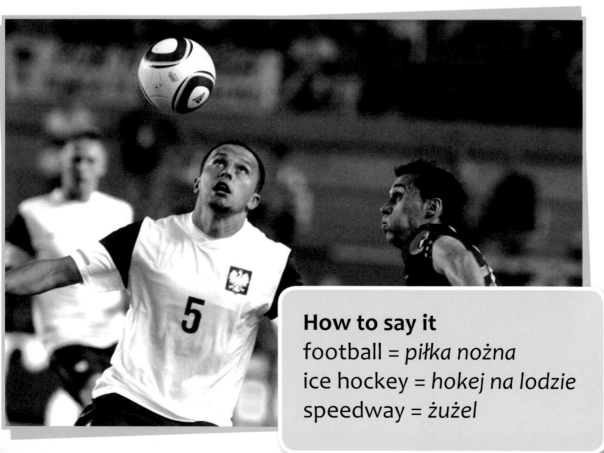

How to say it
football = *piłka nożna*
ice hockey = *hokej na lodzie*
speedway = *żużel*

Dances from long ago are popular in Poland. People all over the world like to learn these dances. They include the *mazurek*, a lively dance, and the *polonez*, a slower dance.

Polish food usually contains lots of meat, vegetables, and cream. A popular Polish food is the *pierogi*. This is a baked dumpling stuffed with potato and cheese, and other food, such as mushrooms.

How to say it
potato = *kartofel*
cheese = *ser*
mushrooms = *grzyby*

cheesecake

How to say it
cake = *ciasto*
meat = *mięso*
cabbage = *kapusta*

Another Polish favourite food is *bigos*, a stew made of meat and cabbage. Polish desserts include cheesecake and apple tarts.

27

Clothes and shopping

Years ago women in Poland wore flowered dresses and bead necklaces. Men wore embroidered jackets. Today, Polish people wear modern clothes such as jeans.

How to say it
dress = *suknia*
jacket = *marynarka*
jeans = *dżinsy*
necklace = *naszyjnik*

How to say it

market – rynek

shopping centre = *centrum handlowe*

Some people in Poland shop in village markets, while others shop in large shopping centres. Polish craftspeople make and sell beautiful jewellery.

Pronunciation guide

English	Polish	Pronunciation
apartment	*mieszkanie*	*MHEE-SHKAH-NHEEH*
brother	*brat*	*BRAHT*
cabbage	*kapusta*	*KAH-PUH-STAH*
cake	*ciasto*	*CHEE-AH-STOH*
cheese	*ser*	*SEHR*
chicken	*kurczę*	*koor-CHAN*
children	*dzieci*	*DZHEE-chee*
city	*miasto*	*MEEAH-STOH*
dancer (female)	*tancerka*	*TAN-THEHR-KAH*
dancer (male)	*tancerz*	*TAN-tsesh*
dress	*suknia*	*SOOK-neeah*
farm	*gospodarstwo*	*gos-poh-DAR-stvoh*
father	*ojciec*	*oy-CHETS*
football	*piłka nożna*	*PEEW-kah NOSH-nah*
fun	*zabawa*	*zah-BAH-vah*
game	*gra*	*grah*
Get well soon	*Wracaj do zdrowia*	*VRA-tsay doh ZDROH-veeah*
goodbye	*do widzenia*	*DOH vee-DZEH-nah*
goodnight	*dobranoc*	*do-BRAH-nots*
hi	*cześć*	*CHESHCH*
history	*historia*	*hee-STOH-reeah*
horse	*koń*	*KOHN*
house	*dom*	*DOHM*
How are you?	*Jak się masz?*	*YAK seh MUSH*
hug	*uścisk*	*OOSEE-tsehsk*
I do not understand	*Nie rozumiem*	*NHEE roh-ZOO-meehm*
I speak Polish	*Mówię po polsku*	*MOO-vieh poh POHL-skooh*
ice hockey	*hokej na lodzie*	*HOH-key nah loh-dzhee*
jacket	*marynarka*	*mah-rih-NAHR-kah*

jeans	*dżinsy*	*DZHEEN-SIH*
kiss	*pocałunek*	*poh-tsah-WOO-nehk*
lamp	*lampa*	*LAM-pah*
languages	*Języki*	*yehn-sih-kih*
market	*rynek*	*RIH-nehk*
mathematics	*matematyka*	*mah-teh-MAH-ti-kah*
meat	*mięso*	*MEEHN-soh*
milk	*mleko*	*MLEH-koh*
mother	*matka*	*MAHT-kah*
mushrooms	*grzyby*	*GZHIH-bih*
music	*muzyka*	*mooh-SIH-kah*
My name is . . .	*Mam na imię . . .*	*MAHM nah EE-meeh*
necklace	*naszyjnik*	*nah-SHIY-kneek*
Pleased to meet you	*Bardzo mi miło*	*BAHR-dzhoh mee MEE-woh*
potato	*kartofel*	*kahr-TOH-fell*
pupil	*uczeń*	*OO-chehn*
school	*szkoła*	*SHKOH-wah*
school bag	*teczka szkolna*	*TEHCH-kah SHKOHL-nah*
shopping centre	*centrum handlowe*	*TSEN-troom hahn-DLOH-veh*
sister	*siostra*	*SIOH-strah*
smile	*uśmiech*	*OOSEEH-meeh*
speedway	*żużel*	*ZHOO-zhehl*
teacher	*nauczyciel*	*nah-oo-CHIH-tzeel*
village	*wioska*	*VYOH-skah*
What is your name?	*Jak masz na imię?*	*YAHK MASH nah EE-meeh*
Where are you from?	*Skąd jesteś?*	*ZKOHNT YEHS-tesh*

Find out more

Books

A Visit to Poland, Vic Parker (Heinemann Library, 2008)
First Polish Words (Oxford University Press, 2009)

Website

kids.nationalgeographic.com/kids/places/find/poland/

Index

Meaning of the words on page 9
lampa = lamp
mleko = milk
matematyka = mathematics
muzyka = music